THE SINS AND WINS OF INCLUSIVE LEADERSHIP

THE SINS AND WINS OF INCLUSIVE LEADERSHIP

a manual for the modern workplace

Inclusive Creation

The 7 Sins & Wins of Inclusive Leadership

Anthony   Sumita   Thor Isak

A manual for the modern workplace

"The inclusion journey can seem daunting"

Allow us to be your guides!

THE PUSHBACK

Katie sees a problem and takes it
as her mission to set you straight

You defend yourself,
I mean who does she think she is?

Katie is giving you an opportunity to become a better leader

Shut up so they don't shut down

"See in 360 degrees. Create a reverse mentoring program to bring fresh perspectives from high potential employees who may or may not have traditional mentorship qualifications"

THE "GOOD FIT"

John wants to hire
the best person for the job

Aother John would fit
in well with the team

Dominika is highy qualified and she brings new perspectives to the team!

Hire the good fit & the good add

"Reporting is supporting! Share diversity and inclusion reports to track your progress in hiring (and retaining!) diverse teams"

THE INVALIDATOR

Jenny is frustrated
with one of her clients

Richard wants to help so he gives Jenny unsolicited advice

Jenny needs to feel heard.
She'll ask for help if she needs it

Validate Vulnerability

"Cool head, warm hearts—build trust by being your most authentic self and create a culture of validation for the entire organisation."

The "Normal" Person

Elaine buys a printer so she can print a picture of her grandson

She tries and tries to get it to work,
but grows so frustrated she
smashes it against the wall

Design for all

If a printer works for Elaine,
it'll work better for everyone

Inclusive design is necessary for some
&
Awesome for everyone

"Make inclusive design work for your workplace. Design products (and work spaces!) customised for one-size-fits-one, not one-size-fits-all."

The Ignored Identity

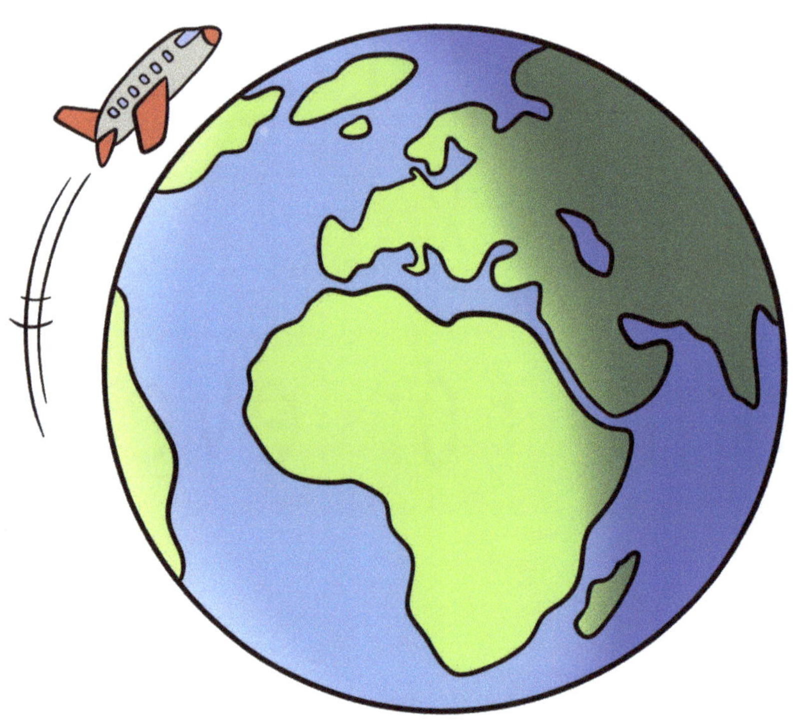

Anita moves her family halfway around the world to start her new job

Anita texts you asking if you can help her find a good school for her daughter before the holiday

See the Whole Person

As an immigrant mother from another culture, her experience is different from yours

See the spectrum; their identity is their humanity

"Resourceful employees are resource-full employees! Form groups that allow employees to connect and celebrate their diverse experiences."

The Diversity Draining

Diversity training is important but some people don't take it seriously

That's not what I mean by unconscious bias
DIVERSITY
Almost made it to inbox zero!

Make Inclusion a Competition

Turn diversity training into inclusion gaming

 The Non-Apology

Anna needs your help
but you ghost her

She's upset, so you say
you're sorry and move on

Apologise to reconcile

A full apology helps resolve the conflict and restore the relationship

Apologise or eulogize your relationships

"Acknowledge the impact. Recognise how a mistake may have affected colleagues, clients, or the organisation. Then open up dialogue to understand how you can be better and do better."

The road ahead
is yours

THE ~~END~~ BEGINNING